Tony Meola

by Mark Stewart

ACKNOWLEDGMENTS

The editors wish to thank Tony Meola for his cooperation in preparing this book.
Thanks also to Integrated Sports International for their assistance.

PHOTO CREDITS

All photos courtesy AP/Wide World Photos, Inc. except the following:

John McDermott/Sports Chrome – Cover, 35, 43
Robert Tringali, Jr./Sports Chrome – 4 top left, 47 top left
Louis A. Raynor/Sports Chrome – 4 bottom right, 6, 27, 39, 47 bottom right
Jeff Carlick/Sports Chrome – 4 center right, 40 bottom right
Tony Meola – 5 center right, 8, 10, 13, 29, 37, 43
Frank Selden – 15
Dan Grogen – 16, 24 bottom left
Mark Stewart – 48

STAFF

Project Coordinator: John Sammis, Cronopio Publishing
Series Design Concept: The Sloan Group
Design and Electronic Page Makeup: Jaffe Enterprises, and
        Digital Communications Services, Inc.

LIBRARY OF CONGRESS CATALOGING-IN-PUBLICATION DATA

Stewart, Mark.
    Tony Meola/ by Mark Stewart.
        p. cm. – (Grolier all-pro biographies)
    Includes index.
    Summary: A brief biography of soccer player Tony Meola, an Italian American who rose to fame
in college soccer and was goalie for the U.S. national soccer team in the 1994 World Cup
competition.
    ISBN 0-516-20181-6 (lib. binding)–ISBN 0-516-26029-4 (pbk.)
    1. Meola, Tony, 1969-   –Juvenile literature. 2. Soccer goalkeepers–United States–Biography–
Juvenile literature. [1. Meola, Tony, 1969-   . 2. Soccer players.] I. Title. II. Series.
GV942.7.M397S84 1996
796.334'092–dc20
(B)   96-17503
                                                                                                                       CIP
                                                                                                                        AC

Grolier ALL-PRO Biographies™

Tony Meola

by

Mark Stewart

CHILDREN'S PRESS®
A Division of Grolier Publishing
New York • London • Hong Kong • Sydney
Danbury, Connecticut

Contents

Who

Am I?

In most parts of the United States, kids dream about becoming a basketball, baseball, or football star. In my hometown, the children dreamed about growing up to play soccer. I was one of those dreamers. My name is Tony Meola, and this is my story . . . "

"In my hometown, the children dreamed about growing up to play soccer."

Growing Up

Tony Meola was the second child of Vincent and Maria Meola, who came to the United States from Avellino, Italy. Tony's father was an excellent soccer player. In fact, he had been a fullback for the Avellino club, which played in the Italian Second Division. He could think of no better place to raise his children than in Kearney, New Jersey, where immigrant families from Italy, Scotland, Ireland, Portugal, Spain, and other countries had been living for years. Naturally, the favorite sport in the neighborhood was soccer, which is the most popular sport in Europe and South America.

As soon as little Tony could stand, he was kicking a ball around. By the time he was eight years old, he was crazy about soccer. Tony's father often would take him to

Tony in the fourth grade

professional soccer games at Giants Stadium, which was just a few minutes away from the family's barbershop. There they would watch the New York Cosmos. The Cosmos were members of the North American Soccer League (NASL), and they had some of the world's best players, including Franz Beckenbauer, Giorgio Chinaglia, Carlos Alberto, and the best player of all, Pelé. One of Tony's favorite players was Shep Messing, a daring, cat-quick goalie. Although Messing did not get to run up and down the field like the other players, he always looked like he was having a lot of fun.

Tony's uncle played briefly for the Cosmos. During that time, Tony got to meet many of his soccer heroes face-to-face. That really made him a big shot in Kearney! And that was important to Tony, because his friends did not consider him a very good soccer player.

"The coach just stuck me in goal because he thought I was fat and couldn't run," Tony remembers. "None of the kids ever wanted to go in goal because they wouldn't get to run around. But I liked being the team's last defense."

Tony's favorite player was goalie Shep Messing.

9

Tony makes a wish.

Tony gradually accepted his role as goalie, and began to work on the skills required to play the position. He practiced diving, jumping, catching, throwing, and kicking. After a while, Tony began to notice something very interesting. The better he got at stopping the other team from scoring, the better his teammates played when the ball went the other way. Their confidence in Tony enabled them to take more risks and be more aggressive. They knew that if they made a mistake, their goalie would be able to cover for them. Tony liked the idea of "controlling" a game in this way.

Tony also liked going to school. He was one of many children whose parents had come to the United States from other parts of the world. Tony developed an understanding of different cultures that would help him immensely when he became an international soccer star. In the classroom, he excelled in subjects such as math and reading, but he sometimes struggled with history. Tony found it difficult to memorize facts about so many people and dates and places. He often had to read his textbooks two or three times! Later in life, Tony saw the importance of knowing about history. He grew to understand that knowing what happened in the past makes it easier to figure out what is going on in the world today.

When Tony was not playing sports or doing his schoolwork, the thing he liked to do most of all was read. His favorite books were Hardy Boys mysteries, stories about two brothers who solved mysteries and crimes. Tony also knew how important it was to have good reading skills. "Reading is probably the most important thing you'll learn in your life," he says. "It is very difficult to function in everyday life if you cannot read, so you should never take reading for granted. Remember, the better you read, the more knowledge you can acquire over your lifetime. And I've always said, people can take away your car or your house or your money. But they can never take away what you know."

Tony's favorite class was gym, and his favorite teacher was Mr. Sprague. Tony thought Mr. Sprague was the most incredible athlete he had ever seen. He could play every sport, and he inspired Tony to do the same. With Mr. Sprague's help,

Tony got his weight under control and improved his footwork and coordination. Suddenly, Tony was one of the best athletes in his class. And by the time he enrolled at Kearney High School, Tony had his sights set on becoming the star of the soccer, basketball, and baseball teams. He would eventually achieve all of these goals.

In the fall of his freshman year, Tony tried out for the soccer team, which was one of the best high-school squads in the country. He made the team, and so did his best friend, Sal Rosamillia. Unfortunately, both Tony and Sal played goalie. Coach John Millar could not decide which of the two should be the starter. He solved this problem by playing Tony in the first half of games, and Sal in the second half. The experiment worked, as Kearney had a perfect 24–0 record and won the state championship. The freshman goalies were a big part of the team's success. So was senior John Harkes, who was voted High School Player of the Year. He would later become the first American soccer player to star in a major European soccer league.

By the time Tony was a senior, he had become one of the finest athletes in New Jersey. He earned all-state honors three times as a baseball player, and the pro scouts who watched him play agreed he had the potential to reach the major leagues. The highlight of Tony's baseball career at Kearney High was when he and Sal hit back-to-back homers against Lakeland to lead the team to the sectional title. Tony captained the Kearney basketball team, too. He was a smart, rugged rebounder and a top scorer. And, of course, Tony was a soccer superstar, earning High School Player of the Year honors just as Harkes had three years earlier. What made this achievement so remarkable is that Tony did not win the award as a goalie. Desperate to strengthen the team's mediocre offense, coach Millar asked Tony to move to the striker position. Incredibly, Tony scored 33 goals! He received scholarship offers from more than 60 major universities— some for baseball, some for soccer, and many for both. Eventually, he decided to attend the University of Virginia.

Tony makes a save for the young Scots Americans in their 1987 game against the Celtic Boys from Ireland.

College

Tony Meola chose the University of Virginia for two reasons: it had an excellent soccer program, and it was one of the best schools on the East Coast. Tony had no doubt that he would make a career for himself in soccer, but he also wanted a great education. Before he arrived at the Charlottesville campus, however, he would get his first taste of international competition. In the summer of 1987, Tony was selected as the starting goaltender by the U.S. under-20 team, which competed in the Junior World Cup in Chile. He loved the experience, and he vowed to one day become the goalie for Team USA in the World Cup. One thing Tony realized during the tournament was that he had a lot to learn about his position. The other young goalkeepers really knew what they were doing, while Tony got by mainly on his instincts and physical ability.

Virginia coach Bruce Arena agreed. Although he believed that Tony had the makings of a world-class goalie, Arena told him that his technique needed a lot of work. So all through his

Years

freshman year, Tony worked tirelessly on every part of his game. By season's end, he had led the Cavaliers to the Atlantic Coast Conference championship with 11 shutouts and a goals-against average of only 0.31 per game! For his incredible effort, Tony was voted to the 1988 All-America team. The coaches of Team USA were so impressed that they selected him to play in a match against Ecuador on June 10, 1988—his first action as a member of the national team.

In the spring of his freshman year, Tony was invited to play for Team USA in a big game at Giants Stadium. He shut out Peru 3-0, as thousands of fans from his hometown of Kearney cheered him on. Coach Bob Gansler was impressed by his performance, and asked if he would be willing to play for the team in the future. Tony said he would, although he knew it would not be easy playing both for Virginia and Team USA.

The following fall, Tony and the Cavaliers were unstoppable, as he allowed less than half a goal per game and earned All-America honors for the second year in a row. But at the same time, coach Gansler wanted Tony to play for his team, too. Tony tried his best to juggle his schedule—and logged a lot of miles flying from game to game—but he knew that, sooner or later, he would

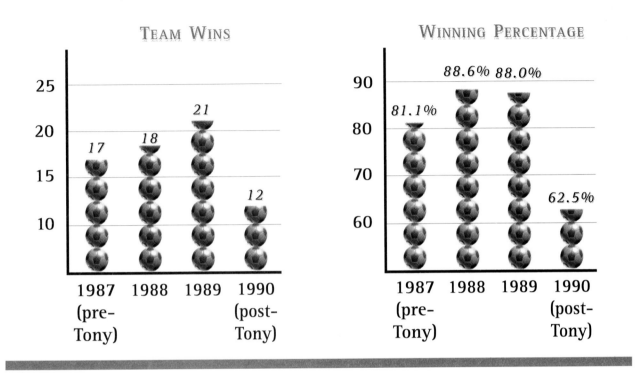

TEAM WINS

WINNING PERCENTAGE

have to choose between playing for his school and playing for his country.

Tony's final college game was the 1989 NCAA title game against Santa Clara. The score was tied 1–1 after regulation, and neither team could score in overtime, so the two schools had to share the national championship. It was clear to Tony that he had nothing left to prove in college. He decided to leave school and devote himself to soccer's ultimate quest: becoming a World Cup star.

The Story

Soccer is the most popular team sport in the world. Yet in the United States, it has always lagged behind football, basketball, and baseball. A big reason for this is that there has never been a professional soccer league to rival the NFL, NBA,

The 1990 United States team that qualified for the World Cup started Tony (yellow jersey) in goal.

and Major League Baseball. In most other countries, pro soccer is the number-one sport, and the best young athletes want to become soccer stars. In the United States, the top athletes usually choose to play other games. Naturally, this has caused major problems when it comes to fielding a world-class soccer team. In fact, from 1954 to 1986, the United States failed to make it out of the qualifying round for the World Cup!

Shortly after Tony Meola completed his first year in college, FIFA—the organizing body of international soccer—announced that the United States had been awarded the honor of hosting the 1994 World Cup. For Tony, this was very exciting news. He had always wanted to play in the World Cup, but he knew that the national team (Team USA) might never make it. As host country, however, the United States would receive an automatic berth. If Tony could distinguish himself as the nation's top goaltender, he could make his dream come true.

The World Cup is the world championship of soccer, and it is held every four years. To determine which 24 countries will compete, there is a long and difficult qualifying process the year before. Each national team is made up of a country's top professional players—sort of like an All-Star team. Since the United States had no top professional players, Team USA typically was made up of college kids who had no experience against veterans of international competition.

USA
TONY MEOLA

An Italian company produced a set of stickers featuring the 1990 United States World Cup team.

Tony joined Team USA in the qualifying round for World Cup 1990. The team was in the same group as Bermuda, Costa Rica, El Salvador, Guatemela, and Trinidad and Tobago. Midway through the qualifying matches, Tony replaced starter David Vanole. If he could win three of the five remaining games, the United States would secure its first spot in the World Cup in 40 years. Tony was magnificent in a 1–0 win over El Salvador, and then posted two more shutouts. But the team did not score in those two games, meaning Team USA was in a do-or-die situation. Again, Tony came up big by beating Bermuda. Then, in front of 30,000 hostile fans at Trinidad National Stadium he held Trinidad and Tobago scoreless in a 1–0 thriller. Not only had Tony established himself as Team USA's number-one goalie, he was going to the World Cup four years ahead of schedule!

Of course, no one expected the United States to make much of an impact at World Cup '90 in Italy. In fact, the Italian newspapers put the odds of Team USA winning the cup at 500-to-1. But Meola and company made a respectable showing. After getting blown out in the first game, they played tough against the Italians before losing 1–0, then dropped a close 2–1 match to Austria. They may not have won a game, but they gained a little respect and a lot of experience.

When World Cup '94 began, the Americans were ready. Tony had kept busy playing for pro teams in England and the United States, and he had been practicing with Team USA since 1992. He was honored to be named team captain. With 85 appearances—or "caps"—in international competition, he was the logical choice.

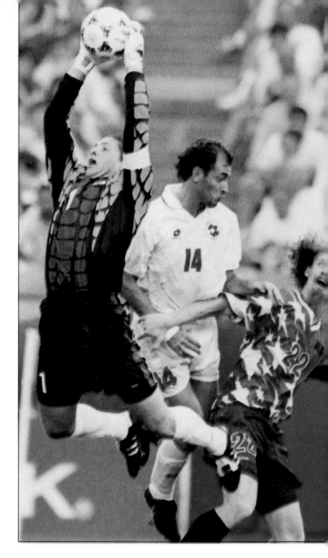

eam USA's first opponent was Switzerland, and the two teams played to a 1–1 tie. Then came the big test: Colombia. Picked by some to win the final, the Colombians were quick and clever. But on this day, the Americans played perfectly and won 2–1 when Colombia's Andres Escobar accidentally kicked the ball into his own net. It was a bizarre way to win, but an important one nonetheless, because it moved Team USA into the second round. There they were eliminated when they lost to Brazil 1–0 on a goal in the 74th minute of play. Meola was

Tony makes a leaping save against Switzerland in an early round of the 1994 World Cup.

heartbroken about the loss, but he felt a little better when the Brazilians went on to win the World Cup. He had held the best team in the world to one goal. And, most importantly, he fulfilled his lifelong dream.

In 1996, Tony signed with Major League Soccer and joined the New York/New Jersey Metrostars. He has now come full circle. Tony plays his home games in Giants Stadium, the same place he watched Pelé and Shep Messing when he was a little kid!

"I finally have the opportunity to play soccer in my home state," he smiles. "It gives all my friends and family a chance to see me play live every week, instead of having to watch me on TV."

Tony and teammate Marcello Balboa console each other after their loss to Brazil.

 Timeline

1989: Named college soccer All-American for second straight season

USA
TONY MEOLA

1990: Leads Team USA to first World Cup appearance in 40 years

1991: Plays in 17 games for Team USA and gives up less than one goal per game

1994:
Defeats
Colombia 2–1
in World Cup

1993: Shuts
out England
with remarkable
performance in
U.S. Cup

1994: Tries
out as
placekicker
for New
York Jets

Game

Tony's game is as much mental as it is physical. "Over the past ten years, I've spent countless hours training and studying tapes of other goalkeepers, so I could become a better goalkeeper myself."

Action!

The United States has reached World Cup competition twice since 1950, and Tony has been the goalie in every one of those games.

Tony wears uniform number one because it is what the world's great goalkeepers have always worn.

Tony says, "I'm really proud of my work ethic. If you want to succeed at anything, you must work hard."

When Tony shut out England's powerful team in 1993, it was the biggest win of his career. He made a string of great saves that soccer fans are still talking about.

People don't realize how hard it is to do this job every single day—but I wouldn't trade it for the world."

Tony and teammate Alexi Lalas go through a difficult practice during the 1994 World Cup.

Tony makes another memorable save.

After World Cup '94, Tony was offered a tryout as a placekicker with the NFL New York Jets.

Tony works hard to keep focused during games. "I don't remember ever getting rattled under pressure."

Tony's 0.34 career goals-against average for the University of Virginia is the best in school history.

Tony keeps his cool against a goal attempt by Brazil's center, Santos.

Dealing

Tony Meola's dream of playing in World Cup '94 was nearly derailed when he reported to the team in 1992 carrying a few extra pounds on his 6' 1" frame. Also reporting were Kasey Keller, who had been playing goal in England, and prospect Brad Friedel. When Tony saw that there were two other goalies on the team ready to take his job, he did not get angry at the coach . . . he got angry at himself. Tony knew it was time to get serious.

"I knew that part of keeping my job meant keeping in peak condition. I'm not one of those guys who can run all day and not get tired, so I've had to work harder on fitness than anyone I know. But my wife and I developed a new training regimen and diet that enabled me to get my body fat down to nine percent."

Tony has to practice hard every day to stay in playing condition.

With It

HOW DOES

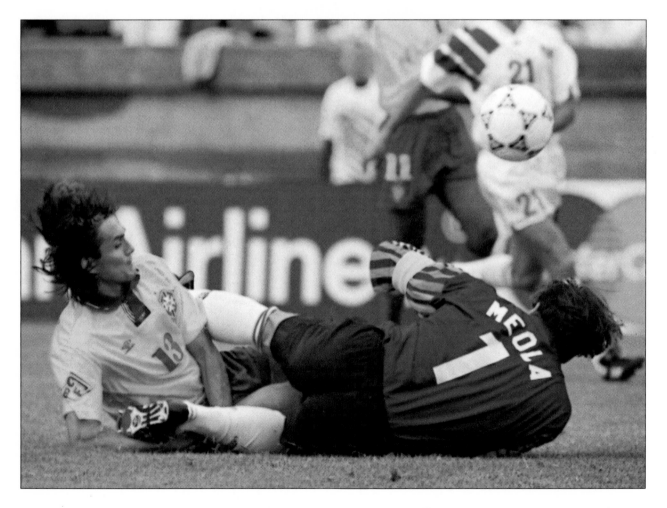

Sometimes Tony has to get dirty to stop a shot on goal.

He Do It?

Tony Meola is known for his ability to come up with miracle saves when it looks like a shooter has him beaten. His secret goes back to his senior year in high school, when he played striker and scored 33 goals.

"By playing on offense I learned what a guy is thinking the instant before he shoots. It became instinctive. Now, when I have to stop a really tough shot, I at least have an idea of where it's going."

Tony often knows where the ball is going before the shot is taken.

Family

Tony Meola met his wife, Colleen, during his junior year at Kearney High School. They were married in 1993. They have two golden retrievers and a python named Monty.

When Tony was a kid, he used to help his father sweep up at his barbershop in East Rutherford, New Jersey. But Vincent Meola always told his son not to go into the hair-cutting business. He wanted Tony to follow his dream and be a soccer star. Tony's mother worked for many years at a company that manufactured envelopes. One of her duties was to drive the company's forklift. As far as young Tony was concerned, you could not have a cooler job. As a special treat, Maria Meola sometimes let Tony ride with her.

Tony stands behind his father, Vincent, and his mother, Maria.

Matters

Tony and Colleen with their "children," Austin and Trevor

Career

Tony Meola will go down in history as the first true world-class soccer player to come from the United States. He is also the finest goalie this country has ever produced. Has he reached his prime? Maybe not. It is hard to imagine that he could play any better, but most goalies keep improving until they reach their 30s. And Tony will not turn 30 until 1999!

Tony was selected the nation's top high-school soccer player in his senior year, despite playing the entire season at a new position!

Tony goes up for a save against Ireland.

Highlights

Tony was a two-time All-American at the University of Virginia. In 1989, he led the Cavaliers to a share of the national championship.

Tony is the best goalie in the history of U.S. soccer.

In 1994, Tony led the U.S. to the second round of the World Cup for the first time in history.

Tony played through an injury during the 1994 World Cup.

Tony was named captain of Team USA in 1993.

In 1989, Tony won the Hermann Trophy and Missouri Athletic Club Award as the NCAA's Player of the Year.

Tony also played baseball for the University of Virginia and was drafted to play baseball for the New York Yankees.

At age 21, Tony was Team USA's starting goalie in the World Cup.

Tony celebrates the Team USA victory against Colombia in the 1994 World Cup.

Reaching

As America's most recognizable soccer player, Tony Meola has been able to make a good living from the sport he loves. But he also knows he has a responsibility to help the game grow.

"I especially like to work with kids. I have my own soccer camps in the summer, and I've done hundreds of clinics around the country for thousands of kids. Aside from soccer, I also work closely with a charity called Do Something, which gives money to kids who think up ways to make their community a better place. I think it's a great way to find the future leaders of our country."

Tony works with Zak Taylor, star of the television show "Home Improvement." Tony has his own soccer camp and conducts hundreds of clinics across the country.

Out

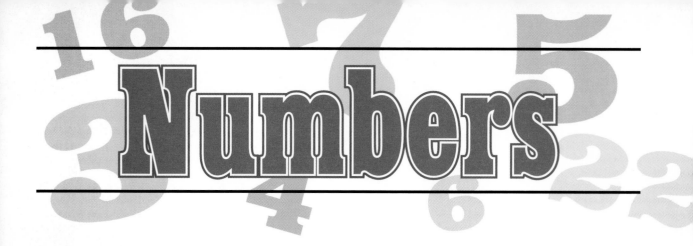

Numbers

Name: Anthony Meola

Born: February 21, 1969

Height: 6' 1"

Teams: Team USA; New York/New Jersey Metrostars

Weight: 205 pounds

Uniform Number: 1

College: University of Virginia

From 1988 to 1994, Tony amassed 89 caps—the most of any goalie in U.S. history.

Year	Team	Games	Goals Against	Average	Wins	Losses	Ties	Shutouts
1988	Team USA	1	1	1.0	0	1	0	0
1989	Team USA	7	1	0.1	4	0	2	6
1990	Team USA	16	25	1.6	4	12	0	3
1991	Team USA	17	15	0.9	7	5	5	6
1992	Team USA	16	20	1.3	5	8	3	5
1993	Team USA	18	24	1.3	7	7	3	7
1994	Team USA	14	13	0.9	5	4	5	4
Totals		89	99	1.1	32	35	18	31

What If...

When I was a kid, I thought it would be very cool to be a sports commentator. When I watched the New York teams on TV, or listened to their games on the radio, it seemed like a fun, interesting job. If I had been forced to give up my sports career, I think I would have tried for a career in broadcasting, because I still would have been around sports. Would I have been any good as a play-by-play man? I think so. I always found that when I set goals for myself, I was able to reach them by working as hard as I could. That was true for soccer, and I think it is true for anything you do in life."

 Glossary

BIZARRE odd; curious; weird

COMPOSED showing complete self-control; quiet; calm; cool

CULTURE the attitudes, traits, and customs of a particular group, race, or country

FIFA (*Fédération Internationale de Football Association*) a group of soccer leagues from many countries that conducts the World Cup tournament

FOOTBALL (or *futbol*) the term used for "soccer" in most countries outside the United States

HOSTILE feeling or showing strong hatred or dislike

INTERNATIONAL reaching beyond the boundaries of the United States

SCHOLARSHIP money given to a student to help pay for schooling

VETERAN one who has a lot of experience

WORK ETHIC a high moral standard maintained while trying to reach a set goal

MEDIOCRE average; ordinary

POTENTIAL the ability to grow or change

PROSPECT someone who is expected to do great things

REGIMEN a regularly scheduled plan of activities

Index

About The Author

Mark Stewart grew up in New York City in the 1960s and 1970s—when the Mets, Jets, and Knicks all had championship teams. As a child, Mark read everything about sports he could lay his hands on. Today, he is one of the busiest sportswriters around. Since 1990, he has written close to 500 sports stories for kids, including profiles on more than 200 athletes, past and present. A graduate of Duke University, Mark served as senior editor of *Racquet*, a national tennis magazine, and was managing editor of *Super News*, a sporting goods industry newspaper. He is the author of every Grolier All-Pro Biography.